CAN WE HAVE OUR BALL BACK, PLEASE?

Gareth Owen was born and raised in Ainsdale,
Lancashire, where his main ambition was to play
inside forward for Everton and England. He left school
at sixteen for the merchant navy, but was invalided
out after falling from a mast in Buenos Aires.
He has had many jobs since, including factory work,
bookselling, teaching, acting, directing
and running a record company.

Gareth performs in schools, reads regularly
for the BBC and for two years presented
Radio 4's long-running *Poetry Please!*.
He now lives in Ludlow, Shropshire.

CAN WE HAVE OUR BALL BACK, PLEASE?

Football Poems
by Gareth Owen

Illustrated by Mike Phillips

MACMILLAN CHILDREN'S BOOKS

First published 2006 by Macmillan Children's Books
a division of Macmillan Publishers Limited
20 New Wharf Road, London N1 9RR
Basingstoke and Oxford
Asscociated companies throughout the world
www.panmacmillan.com

ISBN 978-0-330-44048-6

5 7 9 8 6 4

A CIP catalogue record for this book is available
from the British Library.

Printed and bound in Great Britain
by Mackays of Chatham plc, Kent.

Contents

Can We Have Our Ball Back, Please?

England gave football to the world
Who, now they've got the knack,
Play it better than we do
And won't let us have it back.

The Commentator

Good afternoon and welcome
To this international
Between England and Holland
Which is being played here today
At 4 Florence Terrace.
And the pitch looks in superb condition
As Danny Markey, the England captain,
Puts England on the attack.
Straight away it's Markey
With a lovely little pass to Beckham,
Beckham back to Markey,
Markey in possession here
Jinking skilfully past the dustbins;
And a neat flick inside the cat there.
What a brilliant player this Markey is
And he's still only nine years old!
Markey to Rooney,
Rooney back to Markey,
Markey is through, he's through,
No, he's been tackled by the drainpipe;
But he's won the ball back brilliantly
And he's advancing on the Dutch keeper,
It must be a goal.
The keeper's off his line
But Markey chips him superbly
And it's a goal!

No!

It's gone into Mrs Spence's next door.

And Markey's going round to ask for his ball back,

It could be the end of this international.

Now the door's opening

And yes, it's Mrs Spence,

Mrs Spence has come to the door.

Wait a minute

She's shaking her head, she is shaking her head,

She's not going to let England have their ball back.

What is the referee going to do?

Markey's coming back looking very dejected,

And he seems to be waiting . . .

He's going back,

Markey is going back for that ball!

What a brilliant and exciting move!

He waited until the front door was closed

And then went back for that ball.
And wait a minute
He's found it, Markey has found that ball,
He has found that ball
And that's wonderful news
For the hundred thousand fans gathered here
Who are showing their appreciation
In no uncertain fashion.
But wait a minute,
The door's opening once more.
It's her, it's Mrs Spence
And she's waving her fist
And shouting something I can't quite understand
But I don't think it's encouragement.
And Markey's off,
He's jinked past her on the outside
Dodging this way and that
With Mrs Spence in hot pursuit.
And he's past her, he's through,
What skills this boy has!
But Mr Spence is there too,
Mr Spence in the sweeper role
With Rover their dog.
Markey's going to have to pull out all the stops now.
He's running straight at him,
And he's down, he's down on all fours!
What is he doing?
And Oh my goodness that was brilliant,
That was absolutely brilliant,

He's dived through Spence's legs;
But he's got him,
This rugged stopper has him by the coat
And Rover's barking in there too;
He'll never get out of this one.
But this is unbelievable!
He's got away
He has got away:
He wriggled out of his coat
And left part of his trousers with Rover.
This boy is real dynamite.
He's over the wall
He's clear
They'll never catch him now.
He's down the yard and on his way
And I don't think we're going to see
Any more of Markey
Until it's safe to come home.

Meteor

A Doomsday meteor is heading this way
End of life as we know it, they say
Please big meteor at least stay away
Till after the match next Saturday.

Practising

One day I'll be a football star
And practice makes perfect they say
So I'm practising hard from dawn till dusk
All the skills that I'll need one day.

I'm practising how to run out on the pitch
How to warm up before the game
And how to clap hands above my head
When the crowd calls out my name.

I'm practising signing my autograph
For the fans who beg me to sign
And how to appeal for corners and throws
When it's me kicked the ball 'cross the line.

And you need to have a flexible face
If you really want to succeed
So I sit in front of the mirror for hours
Pulling all those expressions I'll need;

Like anger and outraged innocence
Despair and pure relief
And that glance at the heavens and shake of the head
When expressing sheer disbelief.

I've been practising how to appeal to the ref
How to stare at him long and hard
And how to master that slow, sad walk
When receiving my first red card.

I've been practising too how to roll when fouled
During drama lessons at school
And spend hours on spectacular high-tariff dives
At the local swimming pool.

And in the back of my exercise book
I practise signing my name
And I know already what I'm going to say
In that interview after the game.

I should be playing for the school today
They want me to play on the wing
But I just haven't got the time you see
Too busy practising.

Street Football

Bang that ball against the wall
Head it at the door
Jink around the baby's pram
Run past the dog and score.

Out of the gate and down the street
Jump on to a train
Dribble down to Goodison
Then dribble home again.

Bounce it on your bony knees
Bounce it on your head
Be a dreamland superstar
Tucked up safe in bed.

Striker

I'm Number 9, I'm a striker
    Striking is my best role
        So when you pick the team Mr Gray
            Why do you stick me in goal?

A goalkeeper's life is lonely
    A goalkeeper's life is sad
        To be a proper keeper, they say
            You need to be halfway mad.

Why make me freeze between the posts
    As a keeper I'm a dud
        I was born to be a striker
            Striking's in my blood.

I've got the speed of a striker
    I can shoot and I'm good in the air,
        I've got the boots and the Nike pads
            I've got the striker's hair.

Striking is what I dream of
    Striking is what I like
        And if you don't pick me as striker
            This striker is going on strike.

The Big Kick-off

It was always like this:
At five to three upon the dot
Dad would whistle us in to join him
Round this centre spot
He'd dug out with his heel
Upon the grainy sand
Of Skegness, Yarmouth or St Ives;
And there the five of us would stand
Beside the sea; heads bowed, silent:
Peter, Debbie, Janet, Merriel
And me. All solemn as you please

Like mourners at some seaside burial
Shivering in our costumes
Still wet and salty from the sea.
And always then he'd make this little speech
A speech that never changed though we
Had heard it countless times before.
This never seemed to bother him at all.
Gravely, as if it were some relic of a saint,
He'd place the plastic beach ball
On the spot and fix us with his eye
And tell us, watch in hand,
How – on parks and fields and stadiums
All across our ancient land –
Other lads were standing just like us;
Footballers we would never know
Rubbing their palms, eagerly awaiting
The season's first shrill blast to blow.
And then we'd count the seconds slowly down
Five – four – three – two – one;
Dad's whistle blew; the ball rolled forward;
Another glorious season had begun.

Thirty years on I find I do the same
A little shame-faced perhaps but that's the way it
    goes
Some things are important in this life
And this, I suppose, is one of those.

Denis Law

I live at 14 Stanhope Street,
Me mum, me dad and me,
And three of us have made a gang,
John Stokes and Trev and me.

Our favourite day is Saturday;
We go Old Trafford way
And wear red colours in our coats
To watch United play.

We always stand behind the goal
In the middle of the roar.
The others come to see the game –
I come for Denis Law.

His red sleeves flap around his wrists,
He's built all thin and raw,
But the toughest backs don't stand a chance
When the ball's near Denis Law.

He's a whiplash when he's in control,
He can swivel like an eel,
And twist and sprint in such a way
It makes defences reel.

And when he's hurtling for the goal
    I know he's got to score.
        Defences may stop normal men –
            They can't stop Denis Law.

            We all race home when full time blows
        To kick a tennis ball,
    And Trafford Park is our backyard,
And the stand is next door's wall.

Old Stokesey shouts, 'I'm Jimmy Greaves,'
    And scores against the door,
        And Trev shouts: 'I'll be Charlton,'
            – But I am Denis Law.

Friday Morning Last Two Lessons is Games Day

We straggle in twos
Down Endbutt Lane to the playing fields
In a gap-toothed murmuring line
Filling the pavement.
Mr Pearson strides out in front
The ball tucked firmly under one arm,
His head bent.

We avoid lamp posts
And young mothers pushing prams:
Sometimes walk gammy-legged in gutters
Or scuffle through damp leaves.
The morning is filled
With laughter-tongued and pottering mongrels;
Old men tending bare borders
Slowly unbend
And lean upon their brooms to watch us pass.
Their wives in flowered pinnies
Peer through the lace curtains
Of unused front rooms.

At the pitch
We change in the old pavilion
That smells of dust and feet
And has knotholes in the boarding.
Someone
From another class
Has left
One
Blue and white sock behind.
The lads shout about other games
And goals and saves and shots
Or row about who'll wear red or blue.
Pearson blows exasperation
Briskly through his whistle,
'Come on lads, let's be having you.'

With eighteen a side
We tear after the ball shouting,
Longing to give it a good clean belt,
Perform some piece of perfection –
Beat three sprawling backs in a mazy dribble,
Race full pelt on to a plate-laid-on pass
And crack it full of hate and zest
Past the diving goalie to bulge the net.
But there is no net
And we have to leg it after the ball
To the allotments by the lane
Before we can take centre
To start the game again.

Afterwards,
Still wearing football socks,
Studded boots slung on my shoulder,
I say 'Tarrah' to Trev
At Station Road and drift home
Playing the game again.
Smoke climbs steep from neat red chimneys;
Babies drool and doze
And laugh at the empty sky.
There is the savour of cabbage and gravy
About the Estate and the flowers do not hear
The great crowd roaring me on.

Ghosts

Footy in the playground
Red sun in the sky
I might play for England
Piggywigs might fly.

Johnny Mars picks Spanner
Andy Platt picks Rose
Johnny Mars picks Henry
Henry picks his nose.

Fifty running girls and boys
Screaming for the ball
One goal is the iron gates
One the lavvy wall.

Ghosts sit in our classroom
Ghosts climb up the stairs
Ghostly rows of children
Upright on our chairs.

Ghosts sit on the school wall
Staring every day
As we crowd to classes
At the end of play.

Promises, Promises

Could bang this beat-up tennis ball
Forever against the playground wall
In those days: it all came easy.

Left or right foot, made no odds to me
Simple as rain, it all came naturally;
Played keepy-uppy till the cows came home;

Once all the way from school to past the aerodrome;
Dominic kept count; brainy kid, face like a gnome,
Called him Einstein; computer for a brain.

Can't say I really liked him. Drove me insane
Sometimes singing my praises too loud; but there again
We all need fans and Dominic was mine.

Tells me, 'One day you'll wear the number nine
Of England on your back.' And I thought, Right. Fine.
And being ten believed it all. Well, wouldn't you?

His belief made *me* believe it must be true.
Brains like his, I thought, let him predict the future too.
Swallowed the story whole. Never stopped to question
    why.

But then one afternoon in late July
I caught our classroom Einstein in a little lie
A lie that tightened bars of doubt about my chest.

If he could tell *one* lie, then what about the rest?
And so that day my dreams came to an end:
The cows came home. And me, I realized;
All Einstein wanted really was a friend.

Saturdays

Real
Genuine
Saturdays
Like marbles
Conkers
Sweet new potatoes
Have their especial season;
Are all morning
With midday at five o'clock.
True Saturdays
Are borrowed from early winter
And the leftovers
Of autumn sunshine days
But separate from days of snow.
The skies dine on dwindles of smoke
Where leafy plots smoulder
With small fires.
Sunday meat is bought
And late
Large, white loaves
From little corner shops.
People passing
Wave over garden walls,
Greengrocers and milkmen are smiled upon
And duly paid.
It is time for the chequered tablecloth

And bowls of soup.
And early on
We set out with some purpose
Through only
Lovely Saturday,
Under skies
Like sun-shot water,
For the leccy train
And the Match in Liverpool.

Winners and Losers

As with football so with life
There's those who can't and those who can
And Jack made one of that numberless race
That critics call an 'also ran'.

Even in schoolyard five-a-sides
With piled-up coats against a wall
When captains dibbed and picked their teams
Jack was always the last they'd call.

With two left feet and boundless zest
He'd stumble round with joyful face
Accepting his classmates' cruel taunts
With tolerance and dogged grace.

In later life became a watcher
Followed his team, come rain or shine
Jack Also Ran would put up the posts
Brew tea half-time or run the line.

Content to cheer the feats of others
Jack would sing their names out loud
Or boo and scream at referees;
Anonymous Jack, Jack in the crowd.

But Jack never thought himself a loser
'We're stars,' he'd say, 'in our way too
For where would all these winners be
Without the likes of me and you?'

Man Marker

'Stick close to that Young,' the Gaffer said
So I stuck to him close as dirt
If I'd got any closer to Alex Young
I'd have ended up inside his shirt.

And Alex Young's only small and light
And I'm built like a privy door
But whenever I slid in to tackle him
He just wasn't there any more.

I covered each blade of Goodison Park
Followed him everywhere
But whenever I went to take the ball
Alex Young was never there.

Get the ball or the man, is how I play
I never really care
But whenever I tried to kick his leg
It never seemed to be there.

He twisted me left, he twisted me right
He left me all of a heap
And that night in bed I could feel my blood
Still twisting in my sleep.

'Stop him, stop him!' the Gaffer screamed
Wringing his hands in despair.
But tell me, how d'you tackle someone
Who doesn't seem to be there?

And after the game in the dressing room
I said, 'Boss it just isn't fair;
To ask me to mark a player
Who isn't even there.'

Lies

Started, I guess, while I was still at Farnborough Road:
Our school team won the West Lancs All-Comers' Shield.
Two years younger than the other lads, I was
the star. Brains in my boots and boss of our midfield.
After the game this scout from Blues takes me aside –
Says I show skill and vision far beyond my years;
Tells Dad he'd like me up at Bellefield for a trial.
Nervous sure – but two quick goals soon calmed my
    fears.

They must have thought I'd done enough because they
    signed me up.
Maybe you read it: *Toffees Sign Up Teenage Star!*
That year I helped the Under Seventeens to win the
    Cup.
I always felt success for me was never far
away; something, somehow I could almost touch.
That's how it was.

         It wasn't long before I played
my first game for the second team – Still just fifteen
remember – a skinny kid at school but still I made
the pass that won the game and hit the upright with
a shot from thirty yards.

                    And then I get the nod;
A Wednesday night it was – before the derby game –
The Boss says, 'Get your boots on son you're in the
    squad.'

A night I never will forget, long as I live.
Ten minutes from the end it looks a goalless game:
Then one of our lads goes down. The Gaffer waves me
    on.
All round the Park the crowd are calling out my name.
The rain pours down; the floodlights glisten on the
    mud;
The ball comes skidding to me through the wet
and greasy pitch. I kill it dead and turn and shoot.
The keeper dives. No hope. The ball is in the net.

But . . .
All this is lies. I never was that good.
My brains were always in my head.
So now I'm sixty-six and old and bald
I write dishonest truths like this instead.

Table Football

Thursday night is Subbuteo night
After Mum clears away the tea
It's been like this since we were seven
For my mate Jimbo and me.

It's the Final of the Champions League
That we'd both rather die than lose
So we play as if our lives were at stake
Jim's Reds against my Blues

But we never seem able to get a result
Each replay ends in a draw
For as soon as one of us goes ahead
The other one equals the score.

We've tried to finish this unending game
More times than I care to mention
Now me, I've got three kids of my own
And Jimbo is drawing his pension.

Staying Up

Mum can I stay up late tonight?
Oh Mum please let me stay
Please let me stay on the sofa with Dad
Watching *Match of the Day*.

Star

Two-Four-Six-Eight
Who do I appreciate?
Er me?

Song of the Shirt

After my weekly bath I'm ironed
Warm and dry and crisp.
They hang me on the dressing-room hook.
Saturday 3 p.m. is my big moment.
Got my name and number on my back

Just so everybody knows who they're shouting for.
Me, that's who.
Oh the cheers as I run out!
My servant thinks it's him they're cheering.
Bless!
Let him think what he likes anyway
Every shirt needs a good hanger they say.

The Saturday Monster

Put my pushchair by the window Mam
For it's Saturday afternoon
And the Saturday monster that sleeps all week
Will be waking up very soon.

Can you hear his great voice roaring Mam?
And the tramp of his ten thousand feet?
Can't you hear the song on his giant tongue
As he lurches down Gwladys Street?

Can't you hear him shouting his name Mam?
Calling out to me soul to soul
And now I can shout his name as well;
It's Goal!
It's Goal!
It's

Gooooooooooooooooal!

Sam the Striker

Sam plays striker for our school
And though he's thin and small
No one can ever catch him
When he's dribbling with the ball.

Nobody knows where he's come from
Nobody knows where he goes
He just appears on the touchline
When the kick-off whistle blows.

He's a terrier in the tackle
He can shoot with either peg
And if a fullback fouls him
I've seen Sam bite his leg.

The rumour is he's homeless
That he lives on scraps from bins
That he sleeps in a shed by the railway
Filled with rags and empty tins.

But once the game has started
Sam rules the field like a king
And 'Come on Sam our Superstar'
Is the song our fans all sing.

But he'll never get picked for England
Although he's the star of our park
For Sam, you see, has floppy ears
A tail, four legs and a bark.

Mascot

Watching my local football team play
Would definitely be more fun
If the other team managed fewer goals
And our team occasionally won.

And I'd certainly enjoy it better if
I was taller than four feet three
So that when we managed not to score
At least I'd be able to see.

And I wish our penguin mascot
Wouldn't act so stupid and sad
And keep his head on till we get home
So no one would know it's my dad.

Internationals

Lined up in the backyard
We both call Wembley
Me and my dad
Pick countries.
This is how it goes:

What team you going to be then?
Can I be anybody?
It's your birthday you be anybody you like.
I'll be England.
I raise my fist and shout,
ENGERLAND-ENGERLAND-ENGERLAND-ENGERLAND!
Except England.
You said I could be anybody.
Except England. I'm always England.
Why are you always England?
It's a 'rule'.
Oh!

Who shall I be then?
You can be anybody you like.
Anybody? I'll be Brazil. Yeah!
I dance round doing the samba,
BRAZIL-BRAZIL-BRAZIL-BRAZIL!
Except Brazil.
Why can't I be Brazil?

44

Because I'm Brazil.
Who says?
The 'rule' says, I'm always Brazil except ...
Except?
Except when I'm England. That's the rule.
Oh!

Who shall I be then?
It's your birthday. Be who you want.
Anybody at all?
Anybody in the whole world.
I'll be Man U.
I jump in the air shouting,
MAN U-MAN U-MAN U-MAN U!
Except Man U.
Why can't I be Man U?
Because it's a club. Clubs don't play countries.
Who says I have to be a country?
The 'rule' says.
Oh!

Think of somebody else.
Anybody?
Anybody in the whole world.
But I can't think of any other countries.
You could be your school team.
Schools can't play countries
Yes they can. It's a 'rule'.
Oh!

I'll be Weld Park Primary Under 9s. Yeah!
WELD PARK PRIMARY UNDER 9s-WELD PARK
    PRIMARY UNDER 9s-WELD PARK PRIMARY UNDER
    9s-WELD PARK PRIMARY UNDER 9s!
So it's Weld Park Primary Under 9s v Brazil at Wembley.

And Weld Park score in the first minute. Yes!
Offside by miles.
Oh come on Dad!
Are you arguing with the ref?
Ref? You can't be Brazil and the ref.
Yes I can. It's a 'rule'.
No it's not.
Yellow card for arguing with the ref.
Oh ref! Diabolical decision.
And it's the red card for Weld Street Primary under 9s.
Aw ref you can't send off a whole team.
Yes I can. It's a 'rule'.
Oh!

Sitting in disgrace upon the bench
I ask him: 'When do *I* get to make the rules?'
'When you're grown up and mature like me, ' he says,
Sliding home England's' winner
And dancing his victory jig around the flower beds
While I make for my birthday cake
And an early bath.

Drac the Keeper

Our goalie's name is Dracula
His flesh is pale as gin
His teeth are sharp as razors
And blood drips down his chin.

Don't foul him in the area
Or he'll drop you on the deck
And pull your shirt off with his fangs
And bite you in the neck.

And when the final whistle blows
He's off without a sound
To take an early bloodbath
In his coffin underground.

Generations

We're always arguing who's the greatest
Footballer there's ever been;
Because I'm young I vote for Rooney;
He's the best I've ever seen.

'How would you know?' pipes up my grandad,
'You never saw Tom Finney play;
Skilful, loyal, fast and honest
Not like these big spoilt kids today.'

My brother's era was the nineties
'When the game was at its best
Young Gazza in his pomp and glory
Towering over all the rest.'

Says Uncle Jack who loves the sixties
'Wish I could travel back in time:
See Tottenham Hotspur win the double
When Jimmy Greaves was in his prime.'

'I watched United in the seventies,'
Says my mother's cousin Paul
Saw the one and only Georgie;
Best player to ever kick a ball.

For Mum and Dad the greatest era
Came with the eighties' England team;
For Mum, Chris Waddle was the hero;
For Dad, Glen Hoddle reigned supreme.

They try to make me think as they do
Mum, Dad, Uncle, Grandad, Brother
But for me it's just a case of:
In one era out the other.

A Funny Old Game

They say that football's a funny old game
It just can't fail to amuse
You don't believe me? Then see how we laugh
When we watch our favourite team lose.

Christmas Present

Wrote my Christmas letter to Santa
In the leafy month of June
If you want a football for Christmas
You can never write too soon.

I pestered my sister every day;
'Do you think my football will come?'
She shrugged and told me to ask my dad
And dad said, 'Ask your mum.'

Oh the months they crawl like snails it seems
And there's hundreds of hours in each day
So I wrote two more letters just in case
My first had gone astray.

But finally Christmas Eve came round
And I tried not to fall asleep
While over the houses and hedges and streets
The snow lay soft and deep.

It was dawn on Christmas morning
When I raised my sleepy head
And saw my football nestling
At the bottom of the bed.

On the roof the sound of reindeer hoofs
Cantering over the snow
And the voice of an old man singing,
'Here we go, here we go, here we go.'

A Dog and His Shirt

Bought my dog, Ralph, a replica shirt last week.
Five leg holes including his tail.
Has his name and number on the back
And across his chest his sponsor:
Woofeebones for Stronger Teeth.
I'm teaching him to sing
Our supporters' song:
'Here we go, here we go.'
He frowns and pants and tries his best
But Ralph's no Einstein in the brain department;
Dogged I'd say; a Trier more than anything.

The fox terrier next door
Now he's miles quicker off the mark.
A real supporter; he's learned already
To wag his tail and chant my dog's name:
'Ralph,' he barks, 'Ralph, Ralph.'

Christmas Dinner with a Football Coach

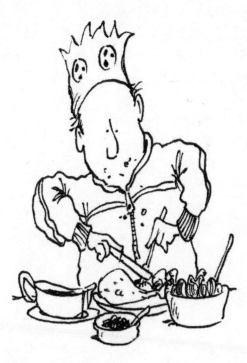

This is the big one.
So get stuck in.
I want to see you up for it.
Want a high tempo but keep the discipline.
I want to see a passing game:
Pass the turkey. Pass it! Pass it!
And use those wings. The wings!

That's it, that's it.
Where were you? You got it on a plate there.
Make yourself available. Stay focused.
Now to me! To me! To me!
And clear it. Clear that plate.
In the hole. The hole.
That's the space between your nose and chin.
Oh you made a mess of that.
You've got to hit the target from there.
Stay tight, tight. Use the channels.
Oh he made a meal of that.
Right the pudding.
You've got to make space.
Remember it's a meal of two halves.

Sports Report

Five o'clock of a Saturday night,
November out of doors,
We sit down to tea,
My family and me,
To hear the football scores.

I'm the one in our family who *tries* to listen
but everybody else just talks and talks and talks.

Dad discusses his rose trees,
Stephen chokes on his bread,
Grandad moans about the cold in his bones
And talks about people who're dead.

Betty dreams about Terry,
'Who's handsome and ever so tall.'
When Mum joins in
There's such a din
You can't hear the scores at all.

Well a few, but the worst is only hearing half a result,
that's very frustrating that is.

Did Fulham win at Fratton Park?
Did Millwall lose at the Den?
What happened to Blackpool at Boothferry Park?
Did Doncaster draw again?

Who dropped a point at Derby?
A fight in the crowd at where?
'There's a terrible draught,
I'm freezing to death
And nobody seems to care.'

Who was sent off at Southampton?
Who was booked at West Ham?
'I'm pleased with that rose.'
'Stop picking your nose.'
'Will somebody pass me the jam?'

The Owls beat the Blades in a derby,
Cardiff beat Carlisle three-nil.
'He looks ever so young
With his hair all long.'
'Will someone fetch Grandad his pill?'

Someone lost at the Valley:
The Orient somehow got four.
'You're not to eat jam with your fingers young man,
You get the knife from the drawer.'

Plymouth Argyle whipped Walsall,
Darlington managed a draw.
'Our Betty, stop dreamin'
And look after Stephen,
He's pouring the sauce on the floor.'

Wrexham romped home at The Racecourse,
The Sandgrounders' winger got three.
'With a touch of compost
And some luck with the frost
We might get some blooms on that tree.'

I've missed Albion and City and Chelsea,
Queen's Park and Chester and Crewe.
'Get your grandad his scarf,
There's no need to laugh
We don't want him dying of flu.'

A sudden reversal at Reading,
A last-minute winner at York.
'Turn down that radio!
D'you hear what I say to you
I can hardly hear myself talk.'

Yes, but you wait till *she* wants to listen to something,
I'm not even allowed to breathe. Just to be awkward
everybody goes quiet when the Scottish results come on.

Those strange-sounding teams up in Scotland,
Kilmarnock and Brechin and Clyde,
And players with names like Macintosh,
MacDonald, McNab and MacBride.

Who wants to know about Berwick
Or Forfar, Stranraer and Dundee,
That Hibernian were humbled at Hampden,
That Stirling slammed Celtic eight-three?

The only thing left to do is go and get the paper.
Trouble is I haven't any money left.

Mum starts clearing the table,
Stacking the plates in the sink.
Would Dad think it funny
If I borrowed some money
To buy the *Sporting Pink*?

While Mum's out of the room he slips me the money.
Have to pay him back of course. He's very strict
about things like that, my dad.

I race through the fog up to Jackson's,
Pumping out breath like steam.
I've got to find out
How United made out
They're my favourite team.

I run my finger down the list of scores looking for the
result.

United, United, United.
Never mind about the rest.
They've won! They've won!
Like they ought to have done
Through a last-minute header from Best.

When your team wins everything's all right.

Shuffle through leaves in the gutter,
Whistle a tune through my teeth,
Tightrope on walls,
Head imaginary balls,
My family's not bad underneath.

Baby Talk

Am six months old.
Big Lady Mamma pushes her big pink face
All in my eyes and nose.
'Say Mamma, Mamma for me,' she says.
'Mamma, Mamma, Mamma,' over and over
When I get it first time round;
What she think I am?
Stupid or something?
I'm not in the mood today for Mamma Mamma.
Big Lady Mamma is disappointed
And goes sulkface to the hairdresser.

Big Man Dadda takes over then
Speakteaching like Big Lady Mamma.
I like the wordnoise his facehole makes.
Better than 'Mamma, Mamma' all the time.
So I say it back over and over very fast.
Big Man Dadda is happypleased
His facehole cracks and goes Haha
Hahaha full blast right in my face.

When Big Lady Mamma comes houseback
With perm all over her head
Big Man Dadda tells her
'He talked. Our baby talked his first words.'
Big Lady Mamma's two eyeholes spout happywater
And her teeth and chest make laughter.
'Who's a clever boy,' Big Lady Mamma says
Smelling of hairsoap and armpitscent.
'Did he say Mamma, Mamma? Did he?
Say it again for Mamma.'
How can I refuse;
I let her have firstwords Big Dadda taught me:
'Come on you Blues!
Come on you Blues!
Come on you Blues!'

Christmas 1914

They cursed his name
With 'Jesus wept'
But into the trench
Sweet Jesus leaped.
They sang of his birth
In voices of stone
The sky was iron
And Earth was bone.
And into the mud
Christ kicked a ball
For Jesus like all men
Loved football.
English and German
Kicked and ran
A game like no other
In the story of man.
Generals at HQ
Were chewing the fat
'An outbreak of peace
Oh we can't have that!'
The general whistled
The brief game ended
And Jesus and ball
Up to heaven ascended.
The players shook hands
Correct and formal
The guns boomed once more;
Life back to normal.

A Roman Soldier Writes Home

I'm with the VI legion and we've marched here from
   Gaul
up to north Britain to build us a wall

which when it's done will stretch, Glory Be,
from the wild North Ocean to the Irish Sea.

Building, I tell you, isn't much fun
for while Hadrian is sipping his wine in the sun

we're working our fingers here down to the bone
slaving for Quintus, whose heart must be stone.

For when we're not lugging great boulders about
we're busy keeping Barbarians out.

My nails are broken my poor bones ache
and our Quintus uses our dinner break

making us play – Oh what could be madder! –
some stupid game with a dead pig's bladder.

It's a game he's invented, a strange kind of war,
where twenty-two legionnaires kick, gouge and
gore

while the winning team is the one who can squeeze
this poor pig's bladder between two trees;

at which, Jove save us, we embrace and kiss!
Can you credit proud Romans behaving like this?

It beggars belief! Still what can we say?
When Centurions say jump we needs must obey.

Kicking pigs' bladders! It just seems so wrong.
Still, one saving grace; it will never catch on.

*In 1973 a vast cache of letters was unearthed near Hadrian's Wall, which told of
the daily life of the garrison there 1,800 years ago.
The above poem is of course an invention, though it is true that the ancient
Romans did play a primitive form of football.

Delusions of Grandeur

Above in the stands the crowd is roaring
Filled with expectancy
And lacing my boots I know I'm the star
Yes it's me that they've all come to see.

Stretch this athlete's body of mine
Watch the slow seconds pass
Kiss for luck the badge on my shirt
Practise my smile in the glass.

Comb strands of hair across my pate
Some dye here and there for the grey
A dab of scented aftershave
A touch of underarm spray.

Studs rattle hard in the concrete tunnel
Feel the excitement rise
Firmly shake each opponent's hand
And note the respect in their eyes.

Wave my arms to the packed arena
Hear the voices shout with glee
And mine is the name they chant loudest of all:
R-e-f-e-r-e-e!

R-e-f-e-r-e-e!

R-e-f-e-r-e-e!

Rivalry

My da told it me
Don't know if it was the truth like
But it's a great story.
Elisha Scott played goal for Liverpool
And Dixie Dean was the Blues' centre forward.
Dixie was magic in the air
Twice a season they met
And he'd have Elisha
Diving all over the place.
Story goes that when they passed each other on the
    street
Dixie would nod in greeting
And out of habit Elisha would fling himself on the
    pavement.

Never Be Another Dixie

Ten, I must have been
When my dad took me to my first game.
Maybe a birthday, I don't know.
Walking the long walk to the ground
From Bankhall Station
Each fifty yard or so
His dicky lungs gave out
And he would have to rest,
Slumping, hunched upon some stranger's wall
Inhaling from his pump
Each desperate, shallow breath.
At ten I was embarrassed;
Wished he'd get on with it
For fear we miss the kick-off.
The ground was like a huge liner
Surprised to be moored
Amongst the huddled, meagre houses.
He saw me to the Boys' Pen
While he stood with the swaying crowd
Behind the goal at Gwladys Street.
Can't remember much about the game
Somebody called McKnight scored;

A diving header at the near post;
One-one I think it ended up.
Once I caught a glimpse of Dad
Struggling amongst the waving arms
To suck the borrowed breath into his lungs.

On the train home I read the programme
Or watched suburban houses
And the golf links flashing by
As he talked endlessly
About the heroes of his youth:
Jimmy Dunn and Critchley
Warney Cresswell, Dixie Dean.
'Never be another like Dixie,'
He said, his eyes on something
Further off than I could understand.
I wasn't listening really
I never did.

And then the other day
I bought a video: History of the Club;
The kind of thing fanatics buy
Who have a taste for history and the game.
And there suddenly, grainy on the screen,
Was the great man in his prime;
William Ralph Dean Esquire in black and white;
Burly and menacing, levering himself on air
To nod another past some jerseyed, hapless keeper.
Then something in the background caught my eye.
A small, smudged figure laughing in the crowd.
The hand raised in exultation
Couldn't hide that face I knew
As his clear breath danced on the air
Rising from uncongested lungs,
Crying 'Goal' to the dark sky
As the headed ball crossed the line
And the white net billowed.

Goodbye, Dixie
(1907–1980)

He died in the stand at Goodison
Died watching a derby game
At the shrine where once ten thousand fans
Hymned the glory of his fame.

And could he have chosen a better place
Or moment in which to die
Than watching us play the old enemy
'Neath a mourning Everton sky?

Yes even a great heart like Dixie's
Must one day cease to sing
But as with death so with football;
Timing is everything.

In a Mist

I really thought we had a chance that year;
One up just before the break
Couldn't see Wolves coming back from that:
Not with the bottle they hadn't got.
Then, just as we were cruising, easy as you like
Into the fifth-round draw,
Off the Mersey and up the Scottie Road
Comes this fog that thinks it's mulligatawny;
Was like somebody pressed the off switch on the day.
The rest was a game for the ears only:
'Here they come.'
'Where?'
'There.'
'Two of theirs?'
'Maybe.'
'There!'
'Who?'
'Look!'
And two ghostly figures loomed panting from the gloom

Before leaping back into the soup once more.
'Who was that?'
'Dunno.'
'One of ours?'
'Could be.'
'What's the score?'
'Search me.'

And maybe – that was it!
What we couldn't see
Became a game that dreamed itself;
A kind of football zen.
Based on the whistle and the cheers
It ended up a four-four draw.
Hope the replay's as good as this;
Best game I never saw.

Success Story

Lost! Lost! And the great dream is over
We slump in the dressing room deflated and sick.
Success snatched away in the very last second
Of the very last minute with the very last kick.

Lost! Lost! And we didn't deserve it.
We fought, driven on by the great crowd's roar.
Lost! Lost! Now we all stare unseeing
At the walls, the windows and the mud-stained floor.

Lost! Lost! No jokes now, no singing,
No flapping of towels, no horseplay, no cheers
Defeat is scored deep in eleven grey faces;
In eleven pairs of eyes blinking back bitter tears.

Lost! Lost! And we all slump like dead men;
Eleven weary bodies drained to the bone
Drained of all energy, drained of all feeling
Eleven sad hearts slowly turning to stone.

Here's a dry crust of comfort for us the defeated;
For me and for you and for all those who've blown it:
The only ones, really, who know what success means
Are the likes of us, who've never once known it.

And Did You Once See Georgie Best?

(After Browning)

And did you once see Georgie Best
And did you take his photograph?
What did he look like? Did he speak?
Did you get his autograph?

When I was five I saw him play
Sitting on my father's knee
I shouted out his name and waved
Did he, I wonder, mention me?

Bill Bluenose

Bill Bluenose up and died last week
Who never missed a game
Come win come lose come rain come shine
He'd be there just the same.

We sang his name the next home game
It soared above Gwladys Street
His ashes in the goalmouth
His scarf on an empty seat.

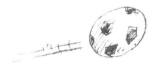

Death of an Old Footballer

He was ready when the whistle blew
Laced up both his boots
Jumped up smiling from the bench
One of life's substitutes.

Raised his arm to the popular end
Flexed the suspect knee
And out of habit showed his studs
To the eternal referee.

St Domingo's, 1878

And didn't the Reverend preach me into a snooze
That never-ending drizzle of a Sunday:
The gaslights on for the dark outside
And the old tobacco smell
Filling my nose off Dad's best suit.
The theme of it's clean gone from me:
Something about women and the worth of rubies;
And I smiled at pretty Alice Parks
Who sat demure among the choristers.
After the final prayer I meant to walk
With her down St Domingo Grove
But found her, arm in arm with some new chap
Her brother says she's sweet on fit to bust.
I watched them strolling off, then made my way

Through Stanley Park, not marking where I went,
Until I came on ten jovial-seeming chaps
Playing at football beside the Stanley House.
Good fellows all, they asked me to join in;
And though I'd hardly played the game before
I kicked and tackled like a thing possessed,
Until the thought of Alice Parks was gone from me.
At dusk they asked me back to play again.
And I think, you know, perhaps I will.
At twenty-one I know I'm starting late
But I had a sense of something new beginning –
On rain-soaked Stanley Park in 1878.

*The first Everton team was formed at the St Domingo's Methodist Church,
Liverpool in 1878.

Tell Me About Your Dream

'Well doctor this dream
    It's always the same see doc;
        Never varies

And always leaves me sweating with fright.
  Talk you through it?
    Well, I'll try.
     I'm at this match, right
     In the crowd like
     And we're all waiting for the teams to emerge
     When suddenly over the speakers
     Comes this voice:
     One of the lads has missed the coach
    So they're a man short.
   Is there anybody out there
  Who's brought his boots along?
 They'd be grateful if he'd play.
What? You have got to be joking.
Of course I've got my boots
Because I know from my dream
That this has some day got to happen.
 In a flash I'm over the barrier
  Down in the changing room.
 ˙ Suddenly famous players
   Are shaking my hand
   And thumping me on the back.
    As they set off down the tunnel
     The manager puts his hand on my arm.
     He looks me in the eye and says,
     'Take the Number 9 shirt
     Wear it with pride lad.'
     And then I'm off
   Up the dark tunnel

To a green field called Glory.
   My studs rattle on the concrete
      My heart's singing
      And the roar of the crowd
      Is like a great beast breathing
      Far away. Far away.
      I come to a wall.
      I don't know whether to go left or right.
      I take the right one
   But the right one
  Turns out to be the wrong one.
 It leads to another long corridor
And another
And another
And another.
The beast has stopped breathing now
 I call out
  But my voice
    Comes back off the endless white walls.
     Then I wake up
      Screaming with fright.
       That's it doc. That's the dream.
       Has it helped to talk about it?
       Well, I suppose it has yeah.
       Do I want to ask any questions?
       Well there is one thing.
       I don't know if you can tell me
       But
      Is this a dream?

A selected list of titles available from Macmillan Children's Books

The prices shown below are correct at the time of going to press. However, Macmillan Publishers reserves the right to show new retail prices on covers, which may differ from those previously advertised.

Give Us a Goal! Paul Cookson	978-0-330-43654-0	£3.99
The Ultimate Football Activity Book Sandy Ransford	978-0-330-44275-6	£4.99
Goal! Alan Durant	978-0-330-44143-8	£5.99

All Pan Macmillan titles can be ordered from our website, www.panmacmillan.com, or from your local bookshop and are also available by post from:

Bookpost, PO Box 29, Douglas, Isle of Man IM99 1BQ
Credit cards accepted. For details:
Telephone: 01624 677237
Fax: 01624 670923
Email: bookshop@enterprise.net
www.bookpost.co.uk

Free postage and packing in the United Kingdom